Baby
Animals
Growing
Up!

Dabble the Duckling

Library of Congress Cataloging-in-Publication Data

Burton, Jane.
      Dabble the duckling / by Jane Burton. — North American ed.
         p.   cm. — (Baby animals growing up)
     Includes index.
     Summary: A photo essay about the first six to eight months in the
life of a duckling, abandoned before hatching and later adopted by a
farmyard hen.
     ISBN 0-8368-0205-5
     1. Ducks—Juvenile literature. 2. Ducks—Development—Juvenile
literature. [1. Ducks. 2. Chickens. 3. Animals—Infancy.]
I. Title. II. Series: Burton, Jane. Baby animals growing up.
SF505.3.B87   1989
636.5'97—dc20   89-11398

This North American edition first published in 1989 by

Gareth Stevens Children's Books
7317 W. Green Tree Road
Milwaukee, Wisconsin 53223, USA

Format © 1989 by Gareth Stevens, Inc. Supplementary text © 1989 by
Gareth Stevens, Inc. Original text and photographs © 1988 by Jane Burton.
First published in Great Britain in 1988 by Macdonald & Co. Ltd.

Editors: Patricia Lantier and Rhoda Irene Sherwood
Cover design: Kate Kriege

Printed in the United States of America

1 2 3 4 5 6 7 8 9 95 94 93 92 91 90 89

**Baby
Animals
Growing
Up!**

Dabble the Duckling

JANE BURTON

Gareth Stevens Children's Books
MILWAUKEE

Dabble was a foundling. She was found when she was still just an egg, lying next to a pond. The egg was put in a special warm box, called an incubator, to see if it would hatch.

Now, a whole month later, Dabble is hatching. Her little pink beak chips out bits of shell in a ring as she turns around inside the egg. Suddenly she bursts the top of the shell off and kicks herself free.

One hour old

Dabble stays in the incubator while she rests. She is already getting stronger and can hold her head up. Her yellow downy feathers are drying, but her legs are still weak and slip out sideways if she tries to stand up.

Three hours old

Dabble's legs are stronger and she can already
stand. Her down is getting
dry and fluffy.

One day old

As soon as Dabble can walk,
she feels hungry and thirsty.
In a warm nursery she eats
and drinks. But Dabble is
not happy. She calls in a
high piping cheep. Nobody
answers.

7

Two days old

Dabble is lonely, all by herself. She needs a mother. Flossie, the white Silkie hen, is motherly, but she has no chicks of her own. She needs a baby.

Dabble and Flossie like each other. Flossie keeps Dabble warm among her feathers, and answers her cheeps with kind clucks.

Dabble's food and water are close to Flossie's nesting box. Dabble runs down some steps to feed. She splashes in her water bowl and messes with her food. Then she runs back up the steps and into the box. The mess stays outside and the nest stays clean and dry.

Rain has made a big puddle. A duckling cannot keep away from water. Soon, Dabble is plastered with mud. She is wet and chilled. Flossie hears her plaintive piping and leaves her nest to call her back into the warm box.

Five days old

Dabble is nearly a happy duckling now.
Flossie has "adopted" her. She takes good
care of Dabble, keeps her warm, and talks to
her. But Flossie is a hen, not a duck, so
Dabble could believe she is a hen, too!
Dabble needs other ducklings to play with.

Two Mallards and a white duckling also
need a mother. They are just the same age
as Dabble, and they all swim together in
their paddling pool.

Dabble is happy with her new brothers
and sister, and Flossie is delighted with her
larger family. She leads them out to look for
things to eat in the grass. All the ducklings
stay in a bunch and follow close behind her.

Seven days old

The ducklings have found a new, clean puddle. Flossie watches them paddling, but stays away; she hates to get her feet wet. Something is already sitting in the puddle. Four large eyes stare at the ducklings. A bit nervous, they stay near the edge.

The stranger doesn't blink, so the ducklings stop worrying. It becomes a bit apprehensive and shifts uneasily as they paddle closer. Bluey, the nearest duckling, sees it when it moves and jabs it with his beak. The toad hops hastily out of the puddle.

Nine days old

Flossie has led her ducklings to the yard.
Dabble and her friends waddle fast now.
But ducklings would rather swim than walk,
so when Flossie takes them near the pond
they quickly run to the edge and plop in.
Flossie stands on one foot with alarm. She
will not go near the edge. She cranes her
neck to watch from a distance. Soon she
sees they are having a lovely time swimming,
bathing, and ducking underwater. Dabble is
dabbling among the floating pond weed.
Flossie stops worrying and lets them play.

While Flossie scratches about near the pond, the ducklings spin excitedly around in little circles on the water like whirligig beetles. Mallard and Bluey even duck underwater.

Soon they all start to bathe. They bob their heads under and flutter their stubby wings to splash water over their backs. After her bath, Dabble hops out onto the parapet. She shakes herself, and the drops fly all around her in a silver shower.

The water is such fun she doesn't want to come out
yet. So in Dabble jumps for another quick splash.
Then out and in again, and again.

   At last Dabble settles down to preen. She works
quickly with her beak all over her body, squeezing the
water out of the feathers and combing them into
place. When she is finished, her clean feathers will
keep her warm and dry, all the better for the washing
and fluffing up they have had.

Three weeks old

Ducklings grow so fast you can almost see them growing! Dabble and White are no longer bright yellow. Their first downy feathers have faded and their adult feathers are sprouting. All the ducklings still like to stay close together, even though they are growing up.

Today it is Flossie's turn to have a bath. A
hen never washes with water; she dry-cleans
her feathers with dust. Flossie knows a good
patch of dry earth, and she goes straight to
it. She scratches the loose earth with her
feet, then rolls around in it, shuffling her
wings and kicking dirt all over herself. She
showers the ducklings too, but they shake
themselves clean. Ducklings only bathe in
water; they never dust-bathe. But they enjoy
eating grit and bits of dead leaves out of
Flossie's bath dust.

Five weeks old

The ducklings have sprouted nearly all their grown-up feathers. They are very pleased whenever it rains. They rush to a puddle and start drinking — they are always quite thirsty!

The ducklings' feathers are waterproof, but Flossie's are not. She heads fast for shelter from the downpour.

When the rain stops, the ducklings dry themselves. Dabble stands on tiptoe as she whirrs the water out of her wings. Then she reaches around to take oil in her beak from a special preen gland above her tail. As she preens, she oils her feathers. The oil keeps her plumage waterproof as well as neat.

Two months old

A duckling's wing feathers are the last part of its plumage to grow. Dabble and White are fully winged now and are ready to take off. Mallard and Bluey have already flown to join the wild Mallards on a nearby lake.

Ducks like the Mallards and Dabble are called dabbling ducks; they feed by dabbling with their beaks among the mud and weeds of ponds. They gobble up insects and seeds and spit out the mud. In deeper water, Dabble upends so she can reach the bottom of the pond.

Six months old

White has now flown away, but in her place
there is a very handsome silver drake who has
come to be Dabble's mate. At first Dabble is
not sure she likes Silver. When he swims over
to her, she bites him on the neck, right on his
white collar.

Soon Dabble starts to bathe, and Silver has
a good splash too. It is not long before Dabble
accepts Silver.

Now it is nearly winter; the lily pads are turning yellow. In a few weeks all the pond weed will be gone and the pond covered with ice. Silver and Dabble will stay in a pen for the winter, but in the spring Dabble will find a secret place to make her nest and lay her blue-green eggs. Next year she will hatch her own family of little yellow ducklings to swim with her on the pond.

Fun Facts About Ducklings (and Ducks)

1. Ducklings can run, swim, and find food for themselves within 36 hours of hatching.

2. A group of ducklings is called a *brood*.

3. The male duck is called a *drake*.

4. Ducks that do not dive for food are called *dabbling ducks*. They eat mostly wet plants, grasses, rushes, insects, and small animals that they find on or under water.

5. Dabbling ducks feed from the water's surface, usually by tipping up their bodies and putting their heads under water. They can also feed on dry land, and they have the ability to jump from the water directly into flight. Mallards, Pintails, widgeon, Teal, and Shovelers are all dabblers.

6. Diving ducks have long, narrow bills with toothlike edges to hold fish. Dabbling ducks have short, broad bills for easy exploring.

7. The Migratory Bird Treaty, signed by the United States and Canada in 1916, protects ducks and other waterfowl. The treaty requires both countries to manage migratory birds in ways that assure their future as a natural resource.

8. The ability of ducks to return to the same places each year to mate and breed is called homing behavior.

9. The main enemies of young ducks are raccoons, skunks, foxes, crows, gulls, and snapping turtles. Humans also threaten ducks through water pollution, and some ducks even die from accidentally eating lead shotgun pellets left by duck hunters.

For More Information About Animal Life

Listed below are books and magazines that will give you additional interesting information about ducks and ducklings. Check your local library or bookstore to see if they have them or if someone there will order them for you.

Books
A Bathtub for Two. Ball (Todd & Honeywell)
Chuck, the Unlucky Duck. Matthews (Troll)
Dabble Duck. Ellis (Harper & Row Jr.)
Discovering Ducks, Geese, and Swans. Wharton (Franklin Watts)
Downy the Duckling. Johnson (Carolrhoda Books)
The Duck. Royston (Ideals)
The Duck Who Loved Puddles. Pellowski (Troll)
A Duckling is Born. Isenbart (Putnam)
Make Way for Ducklings. McCloskey (Penguin)
A Nest of Wood Ducks. Shaw (Harper & Row Jr.)
Six Little Ducks. Conover (Harper & Row Jr.)
The Ugly Duckling. Andersen (Scholastic)
Wood Duck Baby. Freschet (Putnam)

Magazines
Chickadee
Young Naturalist Foundation
P.O. Box 11314
Des Moines, IA 50340

Owl
Young Naturalist Foundation
P.O. Box 11314
Des Moines, IA 50340

National Geographic World
National Geographic Society
P.O. Box 2330
Washington, DC 20013-9865

Ranger Rick
National Wildlife Federation
8925 Leesburg Pike
Vienna, VA 22184-0001

Things to Do

1. Dabble was a foundling. She was found when she was still just an egg and put into an incubator until she was able to break free.
   Sometimes human babies are born too early, or prematurely, and hospitals have special places to put these tiny babies in order to take good care of them and to watch them closely. What are these special places called? See if you can visit a nearby hospital and learn how the little premature babies are cared for.

2. Try to arrange a trip to a nearby lake or pond where ducks live. Notice how the baby ducklings stay close to their mother. In a paragraph, describe the way the ducklings look, move, and find food. Notice also the sounds they make.

3. Ask your mother or father to take you and a friend to a place where there are ducks and ducklings. Bring bread along to feed them. See how close they will come to you in order to get the good food. They may even walk up the bank all around your feet!

4. Go to the library and look at picture books on ducks. Are there many different kinds or types of ducks? Make a list of the most interesting ones and explain what makes them special.

5. Male and female adult ducks can often be told apart by their color. Do some library research and write a short report on why the coloring of ducks is important.

Things to Talk About

1. At first, Dabble is not a happy duckling because she has been orphaned. Something has happened to her mother. She calls out because she is lonely. When Flossie the hen adopts Dabble, she is much happier. What is it that Flossie does for Dabble that makes her feel loved?

2. When Dabble gets other adopted brothers and a sister, she is even happier. She now has others to play with. What are some of the things you learn by being with other children?

3. Dabble likes to swim so much that she doesn't really want to stop playing. What game or sport do you feel the same way about? Explain why you particularly like this special activity.

4. When Dabble finally leaves the water, she preens and carefully grooms herself. How do you take care of yourself after a long day of playing outside?

5. The little ducklings really enjoy playing in the rain and in the rain puddles. Why is playing in the rain fun?

6. Silver, the handsome drake, has to prove himself to Dabble before she will accept him as her mate. How do children try to persuade other children to like them when they are new in the neighborhood or school?

7. Dabble stays close to her siblings until she is old enough to be completely on her own. Why is it also important for humans to stay close to their brothers and sisters?

Glossary of New Words

apprehensive: fearful, nervous, or anxious

beak: the bill of a bird

crane: to stretch the neck, in order to see something; also the name of a large wading bird

dabble: to play by dipping, splashing, or sprinkling in water

down: the soft, fine feathers of young birds

drake: a male duck

foundling: a baby who has been abandoned and whose parents are unknown

grit: coarse particles of sand, dirt, etc.

hastily: quickly; hurriedly

hatch: the successful effort of a baby animal to break free from its egg

incubator: an artificially heated area, space, or container used for hatching eggs

jab: to poke or punch in a quick manner

Mallard: a common wild duck

nursery: a special place set apart for baby animals to play and grow safely

parapet: a low wall or railing

plaintive: very sad or sorrowful

plumage: the feathers of a bird

preen: in relation to birds, to clean and trim the feathers with the beak

Index